Life is short, full of trouble, and a waste of time!

Unless...

V.C. "CHUCK" WILEY

ISBN 978-1-0980-1997-6 (paperback)
ISBN 978-1-0980-1998-3 (digital)

Christian Faith Publishing, Inc.
832 Park Avenue
Meadville, PA 16335
www.christianfaithpublishing.com

Printed in the United States of America

CONTENTS

Part 2

INTRODUCTION

If this short life, with all the pain, sorrow, and heartache that we all experience is all there is… then maybe life is a waste of time and not worth living! This measure of time we have here on Earth is so short and, even with all of the "positive" things we may experience, there is so much misery! John Watson very wisely observed that we should, *"Be kind; everyone you meet is fighting a hard battle!"*

So why are we here and how did we get here in the first place? What happens when we die? Is that it? If our existence is just an accident of "nature," then perhaps we are nothing and our lives are a waste of time. But hold everything! Maybe there is something that would make it all worthwhile. Maybe there is an *unless*!

Part 1 includes eight chapters devoted to theories and ifs (what I call Th-ifs), some of my thoughts on human intelligence, mankind's insecurity, and what the world offers. Part 2 includes several chapters devoted to the *unless*, which provides us hope for both the present and future life.

My sincere desire is that the ideas and thoughts presented herein will convict and encourage you to listen to your inner voice…and, thus, to very seriously consider and think deeply about the meaning of this life with which we are blessed. I promise to keep it relatively short and make it an "easy" read. Also, I have very purposely not included a litany of information regarding the theories I have mentioned in this book. There are enough other volumes by others that do that already.

ACKNOWLEDGMENTS

To begin, I must say how very blessed and thankful I am to have been brought up by wonderful Christian parents, Bonam and Vivian Wiley.

They and my two brothers, Robert and Don, and my sister, Judy, made growing up and being together as a family lots of fun. Our parents disciplined and gave us guidance with great love so that maturing into responsible adulthood was a most enjoyable and rewarding experience.

I would also like to thank each of the many friends, pastors, teachers, and folks I have worked with and for over the decades of my life. I have been blessed with and gained much from each of you.

In addition, my heartfelt thank you and sincere gratitude go to the dear friends named below for all of the love, prayers, encouragement, and for the editing comments and suggestions as I worked over the months to complete this book…you all made it better!

Judy Allen, David and Barbara Christa
Diane Crabb, Russell and Julia Mason

PART 1

Th-if's (Theories/If's)
and
Some Other Thoughts

CHAPTER 1

Th-if #1: Earth's Beginning?

We cannot see the end of space even with all of the sophisticated scientific tools we have developed…and have, therefore, determined that there must be no end. In other words, we have decided that space is endless! And yet out of that endless space some (even many who are scientists) tell us that "somehow" our little planet Earth came out of nowhere *(The Big Bang Theory)* and over many years (they say millions or billions) developed an atmosphere, land, and seas, such that plants and animals could also appear, develop, and thrive.

Wow! What a wonderful theory! But wait! I'm not throwing science "under the bus." There actually is factual evidence of many of science's conclusions. However, considering the endlessness of space, to believe that ours is the only planet that just *happened* to come about and develop as we know it takes quite a leap of faith.

Maybe there is more to it…think about it.

CHAPTER 2

Th-if #2:
Beginning of Life?

So then, after the earth (as we know it) just *appeared* out of an endless space and had (or "developed") an accommodating atmosphere, all this plant life and several species of fish, birds, and animals *appeared*. And then they all evolved and kept evolving until they were "just right!" That has been labeled the *Theory of Evolution*.

Wow! Once again that sounds like a good theory and is all pretty amazing. But wait! Could there be more to it…think about it.

CHAPTER 3

Th-if #3:
The Life of Humans?

So now we have a planet (Earth) out of nowhere, thriving with all kinds of plants, fish, birds, and animals that just appeared (again out of nowhere) and evolved to thrive in the planet's environment. Next…hang on! The theory is that some form of this plant/animal life crept out of its happy little home and began to evolve until it finally became what we see as ourselves today—human beings. And we are not just a chunk of material, but we seem to have developed the ability to think, and feel, and actually change our environment. But just where did these things called love and a conscience (inner voice) come from? And why is it that only humans evolved as we have while all of the other living creatures operate by instinct? Boy, oh boy, did we ever evolve! We have also credited that miraculous transformation of ourselves to the *Theory of Evolution*.

Wow! Again that sounds like a good theory and is all pretty amazing. But wait! Could there be more to it…think about it.

CHAPTER 4

Th-if #4:
The End of Humans?

Wait just a minute! Even with all of this spontaneous and miraculous human appearance, development, and evolvement, we seem to be lacking something. History and experience tell us that we only live on this Earth for a little while… and then we are gone (what we call dead!). What a bummer! While there are a lot of great moments in our lives, there is also an awful lot of misery and heartache that each of us experience. So is it really worth it to just live for a short, short time, go through all that we each go through…and then be dead and gone forever? I think not!

Think about it…and please keep reading.

CHAPTER 5

Th-if #5:
Human Intelligence?

Well, yes, we have developed quite a bit over the years. We came up with the wheel, the cotton gin, automobiles, airplanes, rockets, and just lately all kinds of magical electronic stuff. We can make verbal requests/commands to a box (some are named Alexa or Siri) that are programmed to do what we ask. And we've constructed all kinds of robots that can put things together for us. Some have begun to think that these man-made robots would someday take us over. Not to worry! Because of our inordinate dependence on and fascination with all of this AI (artificial intelligence) *we* are instead becoming the robots—which has already led to many negative consequences.

We've even landed a man on the moon and sent spaceships to Mars and beyond. We have made all kinds of medical discoveries that help us live healthier, somewhat longer lives. There seems to be no end to what we can accomplish.

But wait! Are we really that intelligent? The evidence seems to indicate we are not. Even with all that neat stuff we have come up with to make our lives easier and live longer, it looks like (so far anyway) that we are still all going to die…be dead and gone in a relatively short time! Is that all there is? I think not! Each of us is born with an "inner voice" that "tells" us we ought to treat our fellow humans respectfully and that there is more than what we experience in our time on earth. Where do you suppose that comes from?

Give the above some serious thought…and please keep reading.

CHAPTER 6

Th-ifs:
Here's What I'm Thinking!

There are a great many theories and ifs regarding how the world (especially planet Earth) and life (especially human life) came about and developed to become such a habitable place—and such an intelligent species.

If out of the incomprehensible vastness of the universe the Earth just happened to be formed; *if* all the plant and animal life just happened to appear; *if* mankind just happened to evolve from basically nothing to become a living, breathing, thinking, creative being with a conscience…*Wow*! However, the odds of such random, accidental occurrences being factual, as suggested by popular theories, are simply not plausible. (May I add, that there are many others who believe as I do and who have documented such. Please read Chapter 9 for examples.)

But, what do you think? Please consider the preceding…and please keep reading.

CHAPTER 7

Mankind's Insecurity

Over the years I have been privileged to serve both adults and children of all ages in a variety of services (law enforcement, child protective services, the courts, homeless shelters, public schools, churches, boys and girls clubs, and several service-oriented coalitions). In addition, I have served with several well-known large companies leading groups and writing technical manuals to operate and repair the equipment they produced for the military, the US Postal Service, and others for worldwide use.

With all of the above experience, I have observed that how an individual, young or old, deals with life's stressors has much to do with their personal feeling of security. In other words, what they think about themselves, what they think other's think about them, and if they feel secure with their circumstances. If they have mostly positive feelings/thoughts, and, thus, feel secure, they are usually able to handle both positive and negative events in a positive manner. However, those who do not feel good about themselves, do not think others approve of them, and do not feel secure with their circumstances most often have strong feelings of insecurity. And being insecure far too often results in negative consequences—some of which are brought on by others and many of which are self-inflicted.

So, what could be the source of the insecurities that seem to be so rudely inflicted upon mankind? (Animals don't seem to be bothered with it!) First of all, we (mankind) need to accept the fact that we are very easily persuaded to have negative thoughts and beliefs by an unseen (but felt) negative/evil source. This source seems to have convinced us that we are better and more deserving than our earthly circumstances provide, and that we have a right and a need to know more than we do. Those ideas are the cause of great concern, confusion, and insecurities for mankind, and lead us to search for answers in the wrong directions. In addition, such insecurities are the cause of many personal and global conflicts.

Mankind's insecurities have caused far too many not to recognize who and whose we really are. Indeed we seem more and more lost and desperate for answers, often looking in all the wrong places e.g., technology, wealth, status, pleasure, fun, entertainment, etc.

So how do we personally and collectively turn our attention from the negative/evil source in order to combat our/mankind's insecurities? Because at the rate we are going, things don't look too good and we could even say life isn't worth living... *unless*!

Fortunately for us, there is a most wonderful and complete *unless* which is fully described in Part 2.

CHAPTER 8

What the World Offers

From the time of our birth to the time of our death we have a natural need and longing to be held, to love, and to be loved. Most of us are born crying (maybe even screaming!) because we have just been thrust from a really warm and safe place into a cold, cold world…and it's downhill from there! Yes, our mommy's tummy is the warmest, safest, and most loving place imaginable, so it is no wonder that we seem unhappy to have been so rudely evicted!

Actually, we have no choice about whether or not we are born. But what's next? What does the world have to offer us now that we are here? Besides the natural beauty of the earth, with all the wonderful plant and animal life, there really is a lot of neat stuff for us to enjoy—especially in this "modern" age. There are houses and cars and all kinds of children's and grown-up's "toys," and maybe even status or fame and fortune…and we can be literally entertained 24/7! And since so many of us fear growing older, there are tons of products to make us look and even act younger. However, no matter how much "good" you may enjoy, there are lots and lots that we all experience that is very miserable.

Regardless of the positive and negative that any of us may experience, in the end, we're still gonna die...and sooner than we think! And we can't take anything with us when it is "our time!" Yes, this life is so short and it goes really, really fast! Just ask any older person (the older the better!).

Please think about all of this and please read Part 2 *Unless*.

PART 2

Unless…

CHAPTER 9

Is There an Unless?

As it states on the cover of this book, life is short, full of trouble, and a waste of time! *Unless*! So what's the big "*unless*"? Is there really an "*unless*," or *anything,* that could possibly give this short time on Earth meaning and make living worthwhile… even in view of the "Th-ifs" discussed in Part I and Human Intelligence Revisited as discussed in Part 2, Chapter 11?

Actually, I believe there is *something* that makes this life not only worth living, but also glorious that offers both peace now and a wonderful home for all eternity. But let's examine a couple of both past and present practices first!

Over the centuries there have been several who have told us about a Supreme Being, a god or gods, and have written quite a bit of information/ guidelines (words of wisdom) to live by so that we might experience happiness in this life and an eternal "bliss" after death. Still others have made-up "gods" and rules/rituals to live by so that we might have a peaceful experience in this life and earn a place in an eternal heavenly home. However, in all of those cases each of the human founders/leaders of their respective teachings/claims have died physically and have remained dead…while never offering any verifiable evidence to their claims/teachings.

However, there is this one named Jesus, and He is actually the big unless! His virgin birth, purpose in life, death, and *resurrection* from death to life again were all prophesied (predicted) hundreds of years in advance of their actual occurrence…and they have all come about just as prophesied. Really? Perhaps you, as have many others, would question that. But Jesus's birth, life, death, and resurrection were very well documented at the time of their occurrence. Much of it is recorded in the Bible by eyewitnesses, and much of it has been written by other contemporary witnesses during His time on earth. In other words, Jesus's life, and the lives of many of His followers, is supported with historical facts. And actually, there is more documentation on the life of Jesus than on any other historical figure. (Also, all of nature and that still, small voice within each of us "speaks" the truth of His Being/Supremacy.)

In addition to the contemporary witnesses who saw and knew Jesus firsthand, over the centuries many others have also verified the truths of His life. In fact, most recently two very avowed/confirmed atheists set out to disprove the resurrection of Jesus—which would have also made the rest of His claims null and void. However, through very methodical, thorough, investigative, and exhaustive research, based on many reliable and documented witness accounts, both of these people, much to their initial dismay, proved beyond a shadow of doubt that the life, teachings, death and *resurrection* of Jesus are actually true…and not a fabrication as they initially believed and planned to prove! These two persons are C.S. Lewis (1898–1963) and Lee Strobel (1952–). Each one has authored several books describing their research and confirming their findings. For details of their methods and conclusions I would recommend *Mere Christianity* by C.S. Lewis and *The Case for Christ* by Lee Strobel.

Another eye opener is the YouTube video *How Great is our God* by Louie Giglio. In addition, there are first-person accounts from many who have had near-death experiences and were allowed to "visit" heavenly realms/places, and from those who have had experiences with angels under extraordinary circumstances here on Earth.

In view, therefore, of the unquestionable truth of the resurrection of Jesus, we must also accept as truth the *entirety* of His claims and teachings for our lives here on Earth and for our eternal lives after—as *clearly* defined/explained and recorded in the Holy Bible. Thus, we do have hope for a worthwhile, meaningful life while here on Earth, and even a greater promise for an eternal life with Jesus—if we but accept His Father God's invitation. *Yes, indeed, Jesus is the unless!*

Please very seriously consider all of the above, and please read the following sections.

CHAPTER 10

In a Nutshell

Once we realize and accept the truth described in the preceding chapter, we must also accept the words of God the Father and Jesus the Son as revealed to humans of their choosing and recorded in the Bible. First, God is eternal with no beginning and no end. That is something that we mere mortals do not, cannot, will not, and need not understand in this lifetime on Earth! There are so many things that we humans think we should know, and when we can't seem to figure something out we simply make something up and call it a "theory"—and after some time people begin believing the theory is truth. And all the while, all we really need to know in order to live a responsible, pleasing, joyous life on earth and to enjoy eternity with the Father and Son in heaven is recorded very clearly in the Holy Bible.

Please keep thinking about all of this and continue reading the following chapters.

CHAPTER 11

Human Intelligence Revisited

Before we go any further, let's take a closer look at human intelligence. It would seem that we have been constantly advancing and, thus, must be fairly intelligent…especially with all we have accomplished the last few centuries/decades/years. Look how far we have come (refer back to Chapter 5, Th-if #5: Human Intelligence?)! We've come up with all kinds of stuff and made unbelievable discoveries to make life easier, more enjoyable, and, yes, even entertaining (or so it would seem!). We have manipulated nature in many ways that we believe is to our advantage. However, much of the time, the effects of such manipulations are very negative and harmful to all life. Many even try to prove human "abilities" and "mindsets" to conquer nature by trying all kinds of "daredevil" stunts. Many are "successful," but in the end they really haven't made us better or "proved" anything of substance or lasting value.

With the above in mind, think about just a couple of very basic truths.

To begin with, we have not taken very good care of this beautiful earth we were given. Then, throughout all of mankind's history we have not figured out how to get along with each other. Instead, there has been war after war, dispute after dispute, abuse after abuse (in too many ways to mention here). And for the last few years a bunch of us around the globe are simply stockpiling enough weapons (nuclear bombs, etc.) to destroy any group who messes with us! Great!

Then, to help us begin to get along better and to help us be more understanding and acceptable of each other, a handful of very well-meaning folks have developed what we call "social media" designed to bring us together and give everyone a voice. Well, guess what? That has backfired big time. Instead of "social media" it has truly become more of an "anti-social" media where many are "posting" negative and/or hurtful comments, both public and personal. As a result, there are now even more murders, misunderstandings, squabbles, suicides, greed, and all kinds of crimes committed through all of these attempts with technology to make things better. (Please understand that I am not against technology, only its abuse, misuse, and over-reliance on.) And, although our life expectancy may be a little longer than in previous years (due to medical and other related discoveries/advances), we are still going to die in a relatively short time!

We also mistakenly think that we need to know everything, and we mistakenly believe that things should be the way we think they should be. However, just as our young children don't know everything, or need to know everything, neither do we…nor in fact can we! We are God's creation, and He has told us in the word (the Bible) and with the Word (Jesus) all we need to know. He has provided all we need physically, intellectually, emotionally, and spiritually to live this earthly life in a joyous, positive manner…and to experience a rewarding eternal life after.

So then, are we really all that intelligent? Think about it…and please keep reading.

CHAPTER 12

It's All About Love!

The Bible tells us that God *is* love and the evidence of that is overwhelming. First, He created the Earth with all its beauty, different forms of animal and plant life, and resources just for us. Then He created us in His own image and gave us this wonderful Earth as our home. He also, out of love, gave us the choice to love and obey Him of our own free will…and all He asked of us was not to eat the fruit of just one tree in the garden in which He placed us. But then guess what? We very foolishly made the wrong choice right off the bat and ate from the very tree that was forbidden! There were negative consequences for our disobedience, but still He never stopped loving us.

After some time had passed, God then gave us the Ten Commandments and asked us to follow them. Once again, however, we failed to follow those basic guidelines. The blessing for we humans is that in spite of our repeated failures to make the right choices to obey our very creator, He never stopped loving us…*but* there remained a price to pay for our continued disobedience. And then God and His Son Jesus, out of love once again, did the unthinkable! Jesus, the only Son of God, willingly left his heavenly home, was born of a woman, and lived among us as one of us. However, Jesus made all the right choices and followed His Father God's requests.

But remember, there was still a price to pay for the sins (disobedience) that each of us and the rest of humanity have committed against God. So out of a love that is beyond our comprehension, both the Father and the Son agreed that the perfect, sinless Son would pay the awful price for all of humanity's sins, thus making a way for us to spend eternity with them in heaven. And all that was and is asked of us is that we choose to accept this payment for the debt we owe, repent of (turn from) our trespasses (sins), love the Father and Son, and live to serve God.

In addition, God has preserved the Holy Bible to serve as our guide for living a fruitful, joyous life pleasing to Him and to provide us with a history of His loving relationship with mankind. In truth, there can be no greater love than what all has been done for us by our Creator!

Please carefully consider the above and the quotes below.

> For God so *loved* the world, that He gave His only begotten Son, that *whosoever* believeth in Him should not perish, but have everlasting life. (John 3:16)

> For God sent not His Son into the world to condemn the world; but that the world through Him might be saved. (John 3:17)

> You made us for yourself, O Lord, and our hearts are restless until they rest in you. (St. Augustine)

> A lawyer once asked Jesus a question, tempting him, and saying, "Master, which is the great commandment in the law?" Jesus said unto him, *"Thou shalt love the Lord thy God* with all thy heart, and

with all thy soul, and with all thy mind. This is the first and great commandment. And the second is like unto it. *Thou shalt love thy neighbor as thyself. On these two commandments hang all the law and the prophets.*" (Matthew 22:35–40)

From the time of our birth to the time of our death we have a natural need and a longing to be held, to love, and to be loved.

Love Is:

#1. _The greatest gift!_

#2. _The greatest need!_

#3. _The greatest longing!_

#4. **The Answer!**

CHAPTER 13

That None Should Perish (The Reason for It All!)

The following is a duplication of a brochure I wrote several years ago. I am hopeful that you will carefully consider what is written and make the decision for your life that God (through the Holy Spirit) is leading you to make.

- You are alive at this very moment for one of two basic reasons only:

1. **If you have not accepted the free gift of God's salvation through the redemptive sacrifice of his Son Jesus, He is allowing you to continue living in order to have the opportunity to accept His gift—rather than perish because of your sin.**

   But do not forget this one thing, dear friends: With the Lord a day is like a thousand years, and a thousand years are like a day. The Lord is not slow in keeping his promise (to return), as

some understand slowness. He
is patient with you, not want-
ing anyone to perish, but everyone to come to repentance.
(II Peter 3:8–9)

This is good, and pleases God
our Savior, who wants all men
to be saved and to come to a
knowledge of the truth. For
there is one God and one medi-
ator between God and men,
the man Christ Jesus, who gave
himself as a ransom for all men.
(1 Timothy 2:3–6)

2. **If you have accepted God's salvation
through Jesus, you belong to Him and
His desire is that you live in order to
serve Him and to further His Kingdom.**

Do you not know that your
body is a temple of the Holy
Spirit, who is in you, whom
you have received from God?
You are not your own; you were

bought at a price. Therefore, honor God with your body. (1 Corinthians 6:19–20)

Jesus replied: "Love the Lord your God with all your heart and with all your soul and with all your mind. This is the first and greatest commandment. And the second is like it: 'Love your neighbor as yourself'. All the Law and the Prophets hang on these two commandments." (Matthew 22:37–40)

• **Think ahead to the moment of your last breath here on earth (which could occur at any time). No matter how young or old you may be—or how long you may live—when that time comes it will seem like your life was a flash (just ask any older person!). When that last moment does come only one thing will matter—what decision did you make concerning God's offer? Nothing else—not how much money**

you had, not where you have traveled, not what you have accomplished, not how you lived, not how "good" you were—no, in view of eternity, nothing else will matter at all.

Why, you do not even know what will happen tomorrow. What is your life? You are a mist that appears for a little while and then vanishes. (James 4:14)

What good is it for a man to gain the whole world, yet forfeit his soul? (Mark 8:36)

The only things we ever do that are of any real importance are those things that count for eternity.

* **You were created, out of love, by God and for God.**

So God created man in his own image, in the image of God he created him; male and female he created them. (Genesis 1:27)

Lord, thou madest us for thyself, and we can find no rest till we find rest in thee. (St. Augustine)

- **Also out of love, God gave us a free will—and we have each one chosen to rebel and sin against Him.**

For all have sinned and fall short of the glory of God. (Romans 3:23)

As it is written: "There is no one righteous, not even one." (Romans 3:10)

There is a way that seems right to a man, but in the end it leads to death. (Proverbs 14:12)

- **In spite of our sin, and still out of a love far beyond our understanding, God has provided a way for us to return to Him—redeemed from the condemnation of our sin and worthy to spend eternity with Him.**

For God so loved the world that he gave his one and only Son, that whoever believes in him shall not perish but have eternal life. (John 3:16)

But God demonstrates his own love for us in this: While we were still sinners, Christ died for us. (Romans 5:8)

For the wages of sin is death, but the gift of God is eternal life in (through) Christ Jesus our Lord. (Romans 6:23)

- **You may or may not know the person who brought you this brochure. But, whoever it was, they brought it to you**

out of love and care for you and your loved ones—both for your lives now and for the eternal destiny of your souls. If you have already accepted God's gift of eternal life with Him through Jesus, we rejoice with you. If you have not, we pray that you will do so this very day! Please do not wait until it is too late!

It is a dreadful thing to fall into the hands of the living God. (Hebrews 10:31)

They are darkened in their understanding and separated from the life of God because of the ignorance that is in them due to the hardening of their hearts. (Ephesians 4:18)

Then the Lord said, "My Spirit will not contend with man forever." (Genesis 6:3)

- **An ex-president of Notre Dame University, Theodore M. Hesburgh, stated: "Of all valuable things on earth, man is most valuable because he is an end, not a means...he is a res sacre, a sacred thing."**

Please remember that you are precious, sacred, and of much value to God and to many others. If you would like to visit with someone to discuss where you are spiritually, please visit a pastor at a local Christian church. You may also call the Billy Graham Response Center toll free 24/7 at 1-877-247-2426 to speak with someone.

CHAPTER 14

Because We Are Sacred

Several years ago, after reading the quote below by Theodore M. Hesburgh (ex-President of Notre Dame University), I was inspired to write what follows the quote to help us see ourselves and others in a positive manner. It seems, therefore, to be most appropriate to include it herein, and I am hopeful that you will find it thought-provoking and perhaps inspire you to make positive changes in your thoughts and actions as you may be led.

> *Of all valuable things on earth, man is most valuable because he is an end, not a means.*
>
> *...he is a res sacre, a sacred thing... (Theodore M. Hesburgh)*

Each one of us is unique…and blessed!

> *What is man that thou art mindful of him? For thou hast made him a little lower than the angels, and hast crowned him with glory and honor. Thou madest him to have dominion over the works of thy hands: thou hast put all things under his feet.* (Psalms 8:4–6)

1. Remember that life is a precious gift… and *everyone* is precious.

2. Remember, even though each of us has our own unique personalities and gifts, we are all much more alike than different.

3. Regardless of your age or status in life, you have the *right* to be respected by all others...and the *responsibility* to be respectful to all others.

4. You have the right to enjoy freedom and to pursue joy, peace, and happiness...and so does everyone else.

5. Learn to like and to love yourself and others appropriately.

6. Remember that you are very special... and *everyone else* is very *special as well*.

7. Be kind and forgiving to both yourself and to all others.

8. Always do your best and allow others to do their best.

9. Take good care of yourself and strive to grow and to be strong and healthy in every area of your life...physically, intellectually, spiritually, and emotionally.

10. Listen to and learn from your elders… and from your own and other's experience, both positive and negative.

11. It's okay not to know everything…you don't and never will, and neither does nor will anyone else!

12. It's okay for you and others to question things and to ask for help when needed… we all need help at one time or another.

13. Take full responsibility for all of your own thoughts, words, and actions. And remember, there are no good excuses for bad behavior!

14. Do your part to make the world a better place for everyone.

15. Live your life courageously in the spirit of love rather than fear.

16. Surround yourself with who and what will lift you up…not those or that which will bring you down.

17. Say "yes" as much as possible…but say "no" when saying "yes" would not be the best thing for you and/or others.

18. When it would not be in your best interest, or the best interest of others, *do not* go along with the crowd.

19. Be helpful to others as much as possible.

20. Take care of present concerns, but look beyond yourself and the moment.

21. Strive to learn from the past, prepare for the future, and live joyously and peacefully in the present.

22. Remember, none of us has *anything* to do with how we are born. However, each of us has *everything* to do with what we become. Therefore, avoid false pride and prejudice, and don't allow other's pride and/or prejudice to limit your potential.

23. Your life *will be* full of rough times as well as good times. Always remember,

however, that it is not what happens to you, but rather how you respond to what happens to you that is most important.

24. Remember, while technological advances and "things" can enhance our lives somewhat, of much greater importance than material wealth and comfort is how we relate to and treat our fellow human beings.

25. Be reverent toward and a good caretaker of all nature.

26. Remember too, we are all in this together!

Be kind; everyone you meet is fighting a hard battle. (John Watson)

Never doubt that a small group of thoughtful, committed people can change the world. Indeed, it's the only thing that ever has. (Margaret Mead)

Thou shalt love the Lord thy God with all thy heart, and with all thy soul, and with all thy mind and thou shalt love thy neighbor as thyself. (Jesus)

CHAPTER 15

So What Are You Thinking?

Now that you have read through the preceding chapters in this little book and, hopefully, given much consideration to what has been presented, what are *your* thoughts? My hope and sincere prayer is that you may have already established a firm foundation with God the Father through Jesus the Son. If not, my sincere hope and prayer is that, after reading and considering the thoughts and evidence presented herein, you will seriously search your heart further and will come to the realization that this life is very much worth living if you have the relationship with the Creator that He has given us the choice to select.

Please remember that you are precious, sacred, and of much value to God and to many others. If you would like to visit with someone to discuss where you are spiritually, please visit a pastor at a local Christian church. You may also call the Billy Graham Response Center toll free 24/7 at 1-877-247-2426 to speak with someone.

ABOUT THE AUTHOR

Chuck Wiley is a life-long Christian who has been blessed to have served both adults and children of all ages over many decades of his life. That service has included law enforcement, operating an emergency shelter for Child Protective Services, operating a homeless shelter, and teaching in public schools. In addition, he has written parenting material for parents and character development material for children which has been used by several schools and agencies to provide helpful information to thousands. Mr. Wiley has also utilized his material to personally teach classes for the courts, public schools, churches, boys and girls clubs, and the Salvation Army among many others.

Mr. Wiley proudly served four years in the United States Air Force. He attended the University of Texas and has a bachelor of arts in sociology/criminal justice.

CPSIA information can be obtained
at www.ICGtesting.com
Printed in the USA
BVHW040328070320
574412BV00001B/4

9 781098 019976